Reflections In The San Juan Mountains

By

Julie Stephens

To my beloved husband,
Bruce

> *Whatever our souls are made of,*
> *his and mine are the same.*
>
> Emily Brontë

Reflections In the San Juan Mountains
© Copyright, 2009, by Julie Stephens
All rights reserved.
Hands Be Strong Publishing
handsbestrong.com

No part of this book may be used or reproduced in any manner whatsoever without written permission, except in the case of brief quotations embodied in critical articles or reviews

9 8 7 6 5 4 3 2

First Edition October 2009
Second Printing July 2011

ISBN: 978-0-9742680-0-2

Library of Congress Control Number: 2009910864

Printed in the United States of America

Read what others have said about
Reflections In The San Juan Mountains:

These shared moments of awe and wonder and reflection are a balm for the soul, a treasure to delight in, again and again, a very personal, authentic, gift for hearts hungry for nature, friendship, and intimacy with God.

> Susie Wheaton, Christian Educator, St. Alban's Episcopal Church, Arlington, Texas

Every morning as I am walking our Shelties down the road, seeing the sun come over the mountains, the blue crystal clear sky and breathing in crisp clean air, a sense of calm and gratefulness comes over me...I thank God for another day in paradise. This is where I've come to refresh my spirit, read, write, paint, make choices and set goals.

Thank you, Julie for putting this book together. It is beautifully written. Those of us who are familiar with the San Juan's will reminisce with smiles and warm hearts. This book will give others insights into the beauty and awe of nature, which is most rewarding for their souls.

> Amy Pierson- Retired Airline Administrator; creator of Amy's Oat Pillows, Quilted Decor and More

...feeds both the heart and the eye with inspiration and beauty.

> John Stevens, Texas country resident, retired aeronautics writer, two time cancer survivor

A lovely book. A reflection of the Peace, Beauty and Serenity of the San Juan's and the Wonder of Nature. A wonderfully relaxing and spiritual book with beautiful photos and many hidden spiritual gems. A book you will want to keep on your night stand and enjoy in bits and pieces, over and over again.

> Becky Vickers, Lake City Resident and Retired Colorado Department of Transportation Environmental Professional

...it nudges gently at the contemplative dwelling in me and, I expect, in every one of us.

> Rev. John Manahan, Catholic Priest, Pastoral Associate at St. Francis De Sales Parish
> Cincinnati, Ohio
> trying to be contemplative

Even the smallest thing in nature can reflect the wonder and majesty of God's creation. As children need opportunities to explore the natural world, so do we as adults. When we spend time in nature we become refreshed, renewed, and reconnected to this wonder-filled world that was created especially for us. These pictures and words inspire me to take advantage of that experience!

> Terry Powell, Pre-school teacher at the
> River Legacy Nature School,
> Arlington, Texas

This book of yours, Julie, inspires me to seek a deeper relationship with God through the outstanding views of nature that He has provided for me here in the San Juan Mountains. Sometimes every day is so busy that I too late realize that I have missed a rich moment to seek the calm and restorative acts that are reflected by God's handiwork. Your book makes me realize that I must reach out and grasp what is right in front of me and within reach and savor every moment as I grow older in these mountains. I must not wait a minute longer to do so.

> Brenda Rock, current President of the Pioneer Jubilee Women's Club, retired elementary teacher, retired Youth Minister and retired to the San Juan Mountains permanently.
> I will live here forever!

Being a breast cancer survivor and being able to recover from surgery and chemotherapy in the setting of the San Juan Mountains and Lake City, I can relate to the healing power of nature for body and soul that is so well presented in this book. I come here as often as possible to let go of stress and craziness of the business world, rejuvenate and enjoy all the pleasures of the mountains...thank you for sharing and writing.

> Stephanie Pierson, Lake City summer resident and business executive

This delightful little book is a nice way to relax and remember why we spend time in the mountains.

> Linda Matthews, Lake City resident and Owner of Back Country Navigator

Loved the photos – really brings so much of Lake City to life. It is hard to put into words, and/or photos just how beautiful and calming life in the San Juan Mountains can be for those fortunate enough to live or visit here. As some say, "if you are fortunate enough to live in Lake City, you are fortunate enough." For although there are other very beautiful places in the world few can compare to the remoteness and quietness of our town. It is here I feel inspired to give more throughout the community, using the talents given to me.

Julie Stephens has captured this feeling in her words and photos. I hope many are inspired by this book to see the beauty in their own backyards for it is there, you just have to look for it. And when you do find it you can then look for beauty in so many other things previously taken for granted. Don't wait any longer – look, as Julie has done, for the beauty of and in the world.

> Erin Cavit, full-time resident of Lake City

Reflections In The San Juan Mountains

Each of us is here for a brief sojourn; for what purpose he knows not, though he senses it. But without deeper reflection one knows from daily life that one exists for other people.

    Albert Einstein

Forward

Reflections In The San Juan Mountains is intended to be shared and to live where it will be read a little bit at a time and reflected upon.

There's an old saying:
God is a little closer in the mountains

My husband describes coming up to Lake City as detoxing. Exactly. Living almost 9,000 feet above sea level in the midst of this picturesque setting is calming and inspiring to the soul. Our spirits are fed up here as our bodies are cleansed. We breathe air so fresh, that after the rain, you can actually taste the sweetness. Autumn mornings look like scenes in fairytales. Golden aspen leaves become magical, sparkling with frost in the sunlight.

The warm months here are lived outside. It was glorious, September! Folks drew together. Some live here year-round, some have been summer people for decades and new people are always coming and going. Sitting on Bob and Becky's deck, enchanted by the colors of the mid-September aspen, talking in voices more linked to church than a party, it was agreed that it is humbling to be here, especially at this time of the year. The mountain was the guest of honor.

Everyday, each of us has the choice to make it a good day or not, to be encouraging to those we come in contact with or not, to be reflective about the direction of our lives, or not.

I send encouragement to uplift elderly relatives, a friend in the middle of breast cancer treatment, a friend recovering from his second battle with cancer in six months and another friend dealing with unemployment. I talk with a friend who lives with a verbally abusive spouse. Another friend is dealing with the fallout of a mentally ill family member. I hear from another whose mother is dying and another with a sister-in-law near death...

I am resolved to encourage more people with a sense of the healing power I have found in nature.

While cancer and joblessness cannot be cured from enjoying a book, no matter how pretty the pictures, positive imprints on our spirits can make a difference in our lives. While sitting in a garden, you can be absorbed in the natural beauty. That moment can turn into ten and into an hour. The positive impact of that small encounter with nature can be passed on to the cashier or stranger in the street with whom you come in contact. You can smile.

It is my passionate hope that this little book will be of encouragement to all who open it. A command was given for us to "love one another" – I send loving encouragement on each page of this book to you.

This timeless force of nature is indeed a healing source of comfort, insight and regeneration. The mountains, lake, river, wildlife and stars bring a source of wonder. Here, we can be inspired and recharged as we engage in partnership with the elements; the awesome beauty of nature and its power.

Back in cities and towns, it is much more difficult to find a restful place away from our busy lives, heavy traffic, crowds and daily rush.

It is my desire that this little book will offer some of the peace and calm, laughter and encouragement, which surround us up here in the San Juan Mountains and help you to become more reflective.

I also have a website for peaceful encouragement:

http://peace.handsbestrong.com/

re·flec·tion　(rĭ-flĕk′shən)

n.
1. The act of reflecting or the state of being reflected.
2. Something, such as light, radiant heat, sound, or an image, that is reflected.
3.
a. Mental concentration; careful consideration.
b. A thought or an opinion resulting from such consideration.
4. An indirect expression of censure or discredit: a reflection on his integrity.
5. A manifestation or result: Her achievements are a reflection of her courage.

The San Juan Mountains are an extremely steep, jagged mountain range in the Rocky Mountains in southwestern Colorado. The area is highly mineralized (the Colorado Mineral Belt) and figured in the gold and silver mining industry of early Colorado. Major towns, all old mining camps, include Creede, Lake City, Silverton, Ouray, and Telluride. [1]

Though I have been to the other San Juan Mountain towns, it is Lake City that my husband brought me to on our honeymoon in the summer of 1977. It is the Lake City area that is an immense part of our son and daughter's childhoods forever and it is the nature around Lake City where this collection of photographs has been taken over the years.

Thoughts come clearly while one walks.

    Thomas Mann

Solvitur ambulando,
To solve a problem, walk around.

    St. Jerome

Summertime in the American Basin

Well done is better than well said.

    Ben Franklin

    This poppy picture was taken in the Secret Garden which is a little treasure found on Silver Street, catty-cornered from the Presbyterian Church. The only requirements are enjoyment and respectfulness oh, and please close the gate to keep the deer from bellying up to the buffet.

Much gratitude to the loving caretaker:
Brenda Wagner.

Flowers are to the earth as stars are to the heaven.

    Secret Garden Sign

Forgiveness is the fragrance that the violet sheds on the heal that has crushed it.

    Mark Twain

You win one day, you lose the next day, you don't take it personally. You get up every day and go on.

    Hillary Clinton

Do all the good you can, by all the means you can, in all the ways you can, in all the places you can, at all the times you can, to all the people you can, as long as ever you can.

    John Wesley's rule

Wintertime here is like living in a Christmas card.

Mother Nature celebrates the 4th of July with her own red, white and blue! This picture of Red Mountain was taken at Lake San Cristobal. The colors in nature delight me, give me joy!

He who formed the mountains and created the lands, the Lord Almighty is His name.

    Amos 4:13 (paraphrased)

There is a wisdom of the head,
    and a wisdom of the heart.

    Charles Dickens

Lost time is never found again.

    Benjamin Franklin

*Nature is the one place where miracles
not only happen,
but they happen all the time.*

    Thomas Wolfe

By three methods we may learn wisdom: First, by reflection, which is noblest; second, by imitation, which is easiest; and third by experience, which is the bitterest.

    Confucius

God grant me the serenity
To accept the things I cannot change;
Courage to change the things I can;
And wisdom to know the difference.

    Anonymous

Fall seven times, stand up eight.

    Japanese Proverb

I will lift up mine eyes unto the hills, from whence cometh my help.

    Psalm 121:1 (KJV)

The many moods of Crystal Peak

Neighbors compare notes on her aura – "did you see that red glow surrounding Crystal last evening" we greet each other – "snow on Crystal this morning"...what a place for reflection...

Then shall thy light break forth as the morning, and thine, health shall spring forth speedily: and thy righteousness shall go before thee; the glory of the LORD shall be thy reward.

Isaiah 58:8 (KJV)

To be satisfied with a little, is the greatest wisdom; and he that increaseth his riches, increaseth his cares; but a contented mind is a hidden treasure, and trouble findeth it not.

Akhenaton

Every tomorrow has two handles. We can take hold of it with the handle of anxiety or the handle of faith.

    Henry Ward Beecher

Find purpose. Serve others. Be realistic. Set attainable goals according to your abilities and talents.

Follow effective action with quiet reflection. From the quiet reflection will come even more effective action.

    James Levin

Doubt that the stars are fire, doubt that the sun doth move, doubt truth to be a liar, but never doubt I love.

William Shakespeare

The lack of light and air pollution allows us a gift that most of the world is denied. The Milky Way is seen with the naked eye in the San Juan Mountains and falling stars are almost common place. A full moon overflows our valley with enough light to walk around easily without the need for artificial light. Very romantic ~

(Personal journal) January 4, 2007 About 2:30 this morning I heard the wild animal noises again & went on the deck – O my goodness, how beautifully the full moon reflected the snow & lit up the night...so peaceful...just the sound of the water running...no animals...

BUT! We had about 60-70 elk walk through our yard & cross the water up the mountain this morning – fantastic...

It is not uncommon to be asked, "But don't you get bored up here all winter" (especially when they find out that Bruce and I don't have TV!) Not only could I never become uninterested in reading, writing or living in nature but we have varied creative ways to entertain ourselves. Flying over frozen Lake San Cristobal in a hot air balloon was a more extraordinary way to spend a winter afternoon!

You must be the change you wish to see in the world.

 Mohandas Gandhi

Do not dwell in the past, do not dream of the future, concentrate the mind on the present moment.

 Buddha

Dreams are necessary to life.

 Anais Nin

Nature cures—not the physician.

Hippocrates

There is a healing quality to nature when we slow down to observe our environment: taking time to smell the mint growing by the river, lying in a field of clover, watching the clouds take on shapes, enjoying the colors in the sunrise / sunset, listening to a stream, walking in a pine forest, bicycling beside the lake, skipping stones in the river, star gazing, growing a red geranium, a garden full of daisies, reflecting after a strenuous hike or while sitting in a garden...always reflecting...

Sheep Day on Engineer's Pass, elevation 12,800, the high mountain ranchers host a day to pet lambs, go in a sheep camp, see the herds, talk to the ranchers and meet their dogs...all on the Alpine Loop in the beautiful San Juan Mountains.

Nothing Gold Can Stay

Nature's first green is gold,
Her hardest hue to hold.
Her early leaf's a flower;
But only so an hour.
Then leaf subsides to leaf.
So Eden sank to grief,
So dawn goes down to day.
Nothing gold can stay.

-- Robert Frost

This bit of gold was found on the climb around Gold Mountain. We find a quick hike is lovely way to begin our day. Gold Hill is found next to Vickers Dude Ranch.

Most locals refer to the peak as Gold Hill, a few call it Gold Mountain, either is fine. If you are from the flat lands of Texas it's a mountain, if you are from Lake City and surrounded by 14ers it is Gold Hill.

Old age is no place for sissies.

Bette Davis

I take great joy in the vibrant colors of my flowers; which was heightened when a huge black and yellow butterfly emerged to enjoy the bright flora as well. For a half hour I took enormous pleasure in watching this butterfly enjoy my flowers. The mix of color, sunshine and life was exhilarating! Suddenly a blue jay appeared and nipped the butterfly's wing.

I know that it 'was only a butterfly' but I felt a swell of sadness – how quickly things can change -

Keep trying. Failure is a part of life. Only death makes failure permanent. Wonder, ask questions and look for answers – likely somebody else is wondering the same thing.

Happiness is a butterfly, which when pursued, is always just beyond your grasp, but which, if you will sit down quietly, may alight upon you.

Nathaniel Hawthorne

You can turn painful situations around through laughter. If you can find humor in anything, even poverty, you can survive it.

    Bill Cosby

When the first baby laughed for the first time, its laughter broke into a thousand pieces, and they all went skipping about, and that was the beginning of fairies.

    Peter Pan

    Many times creatures both great and small have made me smile; have made me laugh out loud. This marmot's picture was taken in American Basin. Research shows that laughter heals the body and eases painful emotions like worry and stress. Laugh out loud – often!

He will yet fill your mouth with laughter and your lips with shouts of joy.

    Job 8:21 (NIV)

There are no rules for good photographs, there are only good photographs.

    Ansel Adams

Rituals of yoga, walks and reflection will help to rejuvenate your soul.

Make an active decision to have simple daily needs.

The golden autumn up here is like living in an old masters painting ~ The Rio Grande Pyramid, on Hwy 149 about halfway between Creede and Lake City.

Yesterday my husband and I climbed 2,500 feet up the side of a mountain and much of our hike was steep and strenuous causing us to gasp for air, all to reach a place we have been to many times before. Why?

This is a reflective journey. I first remember hearing about Waterdog Lake in one of my husband's many letters during the years before our marriage. (Once upon a time, before personal computers and cell phones, letter writing was the method of regular communication between lovers)

It is not the fast jeep ride of long ago in getting to Waterdog that is inspiring but rather the arduous climb together that is reflective.

One of my favorite parts of the climb is the aspen forest in the autumn. God's Cathedral. Aspen leaves cover the forest floor like confetti. Trees gently rock in unison, creating a soft song and a visible pattern of golden leaves touching each other against the bluest skies. I sit in awe each time we are up here, bending backward, looking upward, taking pictures, trying to seize the day – Carpe diem, my husband, now nowhere in sight, continues upward.

I pick up leaves – very large bright yellow ones, some red with yellow veins and some just the opposite, some multicolored red, yellow and green and some bright-bright orange or yellow with an orange tip. I show the more unusual ones to my husband who would later hand me a long ago used hornet's nest and a delicious smelling piece of pine tree that had fallen off a branch.

After hiking through the first forest there is another exceptional view, especially in late September: the colors of the aspen and the pine green at the foot of so many mountains that are seldom visible at that same time; Red Mountain, Crystal Peak and Uncompahgre Peak's distinctive shape against that blue-blue sky is another place to sit and be still...

In another forest on this journey the aspen leaves are now much thicker, actually soft underfoot like a carpet. We see wildlife up here which has eluded us in the past on this hike. We hear a new noise like an animal in distress but different and finally see two deer running out of the woods, a moment later a third one, smaller and crying for them to wait; not unlike older siblings taunting a younger one. Elk also rush pass so near I feel the ground shake.

I need to stop for a drink, eat my peach, to rest, for another drink, for the half banana I hadn't finished at breakfast, to join my husband on a log, yes, I am VERY tired of walking! Thankfully Waterdog Lake is closer than remembered.

We are all alone up here, as I expected we would be. We eat the picnic lunch I had prepared at 6:00 that morning. Food tastes best outdoors in a pretty spot and Waterdog Lake provides that. We talk about coming up to Waterdog on our honeymoon and the many times later with our children at different growing-up stages and now the two of us again.

Waterdog isn't glorious as she has been in past visits. The aspen leaves by the lake are green and brown. They won't turn pretty this season. The air got too cold too quickly. It is pretty but not gorgeous. I have dreamy, pensive pictures of Waterdog with yellow aspen reflected in blue water; also with snow and pine trees and that sapphire sky and water...but not this year. This isn't Disneyland.

The hike was gorgeous and hard. Today we are stiff and sore. Why do we do it? If you need to ask it cannot be explained sufficiently. We are planning to hike Crystal Peak within a week. It will be harder and longer and even more spectacular and unique.

Above all, do not lose your desire to walk. Every day I walk myself into a state of well-being and walk away from every illness. I have walked myself into my best thoughts, and I know of no thought so burdensome that one cannot walk away from it.

Soren Kierkegaard

If you are seeking creative ideas, go out walking. Angels whisper to a man when he goes for a walk.

Raymond Inmon

The future is something which everyone reaches at the rate of 60 minutes an hour, whatever he does, whoever he is.

    C. S. Lewis

If you watch how nature deals with adversity, continually renewing itself, you can't help but learn.

    Bernie Seigel

Peace begins with a smile.

    Mother Teresa

The sweetest sight in nature is a spotted fawn and the most regal is the mature buck.

Rocky Mountain Columbine
(Aquilegia caerules)

    The white and lavender Columbine was adopted as the official state flower on April 4, 1899 by an act of the General Assembly. In 1925, the General Assembly made it the duty of all citizens to protect this rare species from needless destruction or waste. To further protect this fragile flower, the law prohibits digging or uprooting the flower on public lands. [2]

This bouquet photograph was taken in the summer in American Basin.

    My first moose picture! It was taken in the Deer Lakes area. This is the only kind of shooting I do! Seeing wildlife in their habitat is very special. Spotting this moose, she and I watching each other, was exhilarating! I have been coming up here and hiking all over for over three decades and had never seen a moose up here before this summer.

As the deer pants for streams of water, so I long for you, O God.
    Psalm 42:1

To conquer fear is the beginning of wisdom.
    Bertrand Russell

For every minute you remain angry, you give up sixty seconds of peace of mind.
    Ralph Waldo Emerson

Perhaps the truth depends on a walk around the lake.
    Wallace Stevens

Lake San Cristobal in autumn

You don't take a photograph, you make it.

    Ansel Adams

The aim of art is to represent not the outward appearance of things, but their inward significance.

    Aristotle

Poetry is an echo, asking a shadow to dance.

    Carl Sandburg

    This treasure is found on Nellie Creek Road, on the way to Uncompahgre Peak. The double waterfall demands to be the center of attention, especially in the autumn when surrounded by glowing golden aspen. It never ceases to be stunning... awesomely beautiful and a wonderful place for personal reflection.

    The walk to the double waterfall is less than a half hour starting from the road, a few minutes by vehicle.

What we have done for ourselves alone dies with us; what we have done for others and the world remains and is immortal.

    Albert Pike

Forgive yourself and others. Release your negative energy that holds you back - past failures. Embrace life. An essential component to becoming a wise person is to be aware of how short life is. Perhaps pondering death can bring more appreciation to life. Take time to appreciate the expanse and beauty of your life and our earth.

Give me perspective God...

Realize that money alone cannot help you feel fulfilled.

Remember. Lord how short life is, how frail you have made all flesh.

    Psalm 89:47 (Book of Common Prayer)

The distinctive shape of Uncompahgre Peak

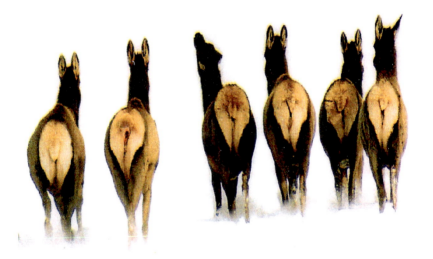

When humor goes, there goes civilization.

Erma Bombeck

Laugh. Laughter is the best medicine! It releases endorphins and promotes longevity.

This picture makes me laugh! In the winter here we would divide the day as above and below zero. I could tell during the night, under the electric blanket, when it dropped below zero as I would awaken feeling as if someone had opened the freezer door in front of me. During the day we couldn't believe how much warmer it felt once we were above zero, still far below freezing, but above zero made a huge difference.

This was taken in January. As usual on my morning walk I had my camera and my thoughts. No one else was living in our valley; even Bob and Becky had taken off for Las Vegas. The wintry air caused my lungs to ache and the metal frames of my glasses were painful against my face. It- was -cold.

The only sound was the crunching of my snow boots against the snow. Suddenly I was aware of being watched. Looking up I saw a dozen elk. I was in delight, in wonderment, in awe. Suddenly, in unison I was mooned!

If we don't change, we don't grow. If we don't grow, we aren't really living.

    Gail Sheehy

The only true wisdom is in knowing you know nothing.

    Socrates

(Personal journal 2006) The morning sky was striped delicately pink and blue - like a baby blanket!!!

For I am the LORD, your God, who takes hold of your right hand and says to you,
Do not fear; I will help you.

    Isaiah 41:13 (NIV)

A Gratitude Journal

Everyone has something to be grateful for. Keep a journal of the good things that have happened to you. If nothing instantly comes to mind, think harder. The secret to being more positive is recognizing the benefits and possibilities of any situation, and understanding that it could always be worse.

If all else fails, think of how life could be worse, and flip the thought process to recognize your blessings. For example: "I don't like school" can turn into "I have the opportunity to go to school, and I can work harder and turn my grades around and ultimately have a better chance at getting a good job which will give me more opportunities." Keep a notebook with daily entries, writing down all your blessings and instead of being negative, read through them and remind yourself of what's going on that is good.

Record your accomplishments as well as your joys. Take time to reflect on what you have previously written. Be inspired. Be an inspiration.

If a fellow isn't thankful for what he's got, he isn't likely to be thankful for what he's going to get.
Frank A. Clark

You are my hiding place; you will protect me from trouble and surround me with songs of deliverance. Selah. (pause and reflect)

Psalm 32:7 (NIV)

My friend Susie sent this Bible quote in part to a response from an e-mail I sent her about the beauty and joy I experience in this place. She was also contemplating taking another friend up on an offer to visit the mountains; in part as an escape from a sadness she was enduring.

I consider myself a spiritual person rather than a religious one. Paulette and I were talking about that recently... not fitting neatly into a doctrine box. Sort of cringing when someone refers to us as a religious person, yet a huge part of thriving up here is being spiritual...

I have recently been surprised in discovering that others up here also attend more than one church as we do. Perhaps more time is taken for spiritual reflection up here in the midst of the mountains, in nature...

*Trust in the LORD with all your heart
and lean not on your own understanding;
in all your ways acknowledge him,
and he will direct your paths.*

Proverbs 3:5-6

Is Happiness Catching?

Research shows that happiness isn't just an individual phenomenon; we can catch happiness like an emotional virus.

I've seen this in action!

I come to work, The General Store these days, ready to work in a very cheery mood. People come up here for the inspiring nature and you don't have to go looking for it – inspiring nature surrounds us in Lake City, Colorado.

In my excited happy demeanor I greet folks and ask how they are doing – most grin and reply in kind – just great! And you?

Fantastic! It's a rule up here – you're only allowed to be doing great! They laugh and we may talk – usually about the simple joys of nature

A few folks may say – ok –

To which I reply – Up here in the beautiful San Juan Mountains!? Just OK? Are you kidding me! Most folks laugh and their outlook improves.

A few may continue with – well, it's cold

Better than the heat most people who come up here are escaping!

They smile and nod, that's true.

Some complain about the rain.

I tell them it's like when we took our kids to the Grand Canyon. This is our time to be here; we put our ponchos on and go outside, besides, the aspen need the rain.

Then they usually reflect on the drought where they came from and agree.

I have been told that I am very kind – people say they like my attitude – that I am the most uplifting person that they have come across lately.

Most of the folks who visit here are on vacation and they deserve to have as happy a stay as possible – but technically, we all are here for a brief stay and might as well be cheerful and inspiring and uplifting!

Reflections in the San Juan Mountains...

Reflections...

Epilogue

In the United States research shows that after making enough money to meet our basic needs: food, shelter, and clothing, that any money we make beyond those basics will have an insignificant effect on our happiness, our comfort level can increase but not our happiness.

Once we make enough money to support our basic needs, our happiness will not be significantly affected by how much money we make, but by our level of optimism. That point has been made even by some growing up in poverty, such as Bill Cosby, as quoted in this book.

I've been called a Pollyanna, but why choose to live in a world that is half empty, dark and sad? Our attitude is our choice. If we don't enjoy the simple, everyday gifts we are given, we are not living a full life.

For me, no career, lovely house or money to buy 'stuff' matters without a well-balanced life that includes a healthy life style, loved ones, a positive, giving spirit and taking time to sit and be still in nature.

Healthy life habits are crucial, and it is appreciation for life's simple gifts that matter most. If we live our lives working weekends instead of enthusiastically attending that little league game, taking the beauty in nature that surrounds us for granted, watching TV instead of taking a walk or engaging in time with our spouse, we are missing out on a full life.

No one is guaranteed tomorrow. Everyday is a choice. Seek balance. We should reflect periodically and make changes where necessary while we still can.

Throughout Ecclesiastes the author mentions that apart from God it is impossible to enjoy the life we have. God gives us satisfaction in our work, in doing good deeds and in having a well balanced life.

What gain have the workers from their toil? I have seen the business that God has given to everyone to be busy with. He has made everything suitable for its time; moreover he has put a sense of past and future into their minds, yet they cannot find out what God has done from the beginning to the end. I know that there is nothing better for them than to be happy and enjoy themselves as long as they live; moreover, it is God's gift that all should eat and drink and take pleasure in all their toil. I know that whatever God does endures forever; nothing can be added to it, nor anything taken from it; God has done this, so that all should stand in awe before him.

Ecclesiastes 3:9-14 (NRSV)

Recommended reading

"Lake City Hiking" by Lyndon Lampert

"Welcome Home" by Perk Vickers

"Walden; or, Life in the Woods" by Henry David Thoreau

Acknowledgements

Thank you to my husband Bruce for his continued love and encouragement and technical support. Thank you to my dear friend Amy the most positive person I know, for her loving, listening ear.

Thank you for those who read first drafts and gave their supportive input: the good, the bad and the ugly.

Thank you to all who have gone before us who have left the world a better place for their reflective thoughts and lives.

The Book of Common Prayer

Note 1: from Wikipedia.com

Note 2: from 50states.com

Thank you to so many of the friends we've made over the years in Lake City who make it such a welcomingly place to live: the Vickers, David and Candy, joyful Dawn, Ed and Mary and the good folks at St. James, Erin and the good folks at St. Rose of Lima, Karen and Beth and the many children I have been privileged to work with –

About the Author

Julie Stephens is a certified teacher with a masters in education and a BFA in theater; she is a self taught, award winning photographer. The Stephens treasure living in nature and relish hiking and bicycling. This picture was taken on the mountain summit of Crystal Peak, 12,923 feet above sea level. They are the proud parents of a grown son and daughter.

May you live each day of your life -

    Jonathan Swift

Notes

Additional copies of
Reflections In the San Juan Mountains
can be obtained from handsbestrong.com

Questions or comments about this material can be directed to: support@handsbestrong.com

May the graciousness of the LORD our God be upon us;
    prosper the work of our hands;
        prosper our handiwork.   Ps 90:17